THE BRIDE OF CHRIST

Ministry Guide

THE BRIDE OF CHRIST

Ministry Guide

A Scripture-Rooted Journey into
the Heart of Divine Love

Symbol & Silence
symbolandsilence.com

ISBN: 978-1-972088-02-9

"I am my beloved's and my beloved is mine."

Song of Solomon 6:3

Table of Contents

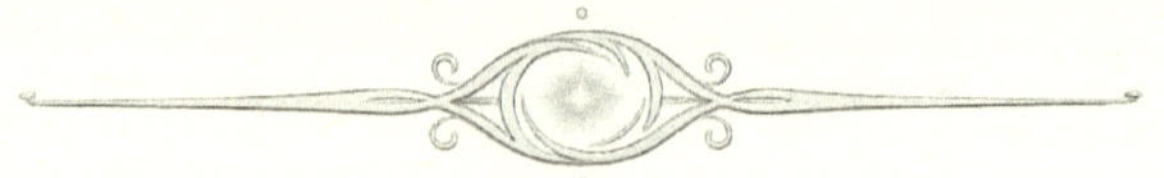

Welcome to the Journey

The Symbol & Silence series, *The Bride of Christ*, invites the Church into a deeper exploration of the Christian life, not merely as belief to affirm or behavior to manage, but as a living relationship unfolding between Christ and His people.

This Ministry Guide is written for pastors, teachers, and ministry leaders who sense that many believers are longing for more than information alone. Beneath faithful attendance and sincere discipleship efforts, many in our congregations quietly hunger for a deeper experience of communion with God. The biblical vision of the Church as the Bride of Christ speaks directly to that longing.

Throughout Scripture, the imagery of covenant, desire, fidelity, and union is not presented as decorative language, but as a window into God's ultimate purpose for His people. In this series, the Bride of Christ is approached not as mere metaphor, but as a formative theological reality that shapes how we understand salvation, discipleship, and spiritual maturity. [1]

This guide is designed to help you lead your people through that journey with clarity and pastoral confidence.

Each movement of the series traces a stage in the Church's preparation:

- awakening to God's desire for His people
- cultivating practices that deepen attentiveness
- gently confronting the barriers that divide the heart
- allowing the Spirit's quiet work of purification
- strengthening an abiding hope in an unfinished world
- orienting the Church toward the joy of union with Christ

At its heart, this series is not merely an instructional curriculum but a formative journey. Many believers are well-practiced in acquiring biblical information, yet still quietly long for a deeper experience of communion with God. [2] The biblical vision of the Church as the Bride of Christ speaks directly into that hunger, offering a framework that is both theologically rich and pastorally restorative.

---

1 See Hosea 2:19–20; Isaiah 54:5; Ephesians 5:25–32; Revelation 19:6–9.

2 Compare John 17:3; 2 Corinthians 3:18.

Throughout the series, the emphasis remains steady: the Christian life is not merely about mastering doctrine or sustaining activity, but about being gradually formed into a people who live in responsive love toward Christ.

Guiding the Congregational Journey

This Ministry Guide is designed to support pastors and ministry leaders as they shepherd their congregations through the theological and spiritual movements of *The Bride of Christ.*

The aim of this resource is to support and enrich the life of the Church. Used alongside the participant materials, this guide equips leaders to preach, teach, and shepherd in ways that help believers move from knowing about God toward a more attentive life with Him.

This guide is intended to assist you in preaching, teaching, and pastorally applying these themes within the ordinary life of your congregation. Each week's material is structured to help you:

- draw out the central biblical movement
- connect the theme to the lived experience of your people
- and shepherd your congregation toward a more attentive life with Christ

The expanded insights and theological reflections are not meant to prescribe a single preaching approach. Rather, they are offered as pastoral scaffolding – a resource to help you prayerfully discern how these themes may best serve your particular church context.

Some congregations may engage the series primarily through preaching. Others may integrate it into small groups, discipleship pathways, or seasonal formation initiatives. The material is intentionally flexible so that you may lead with wisdom appropriate to your setting.

How to Use These Materials

The Bride of Christ – Ministry Guide is designed to support pastors and ministry leaders as they prayerfully lead their congregations through the central movements of this series. The materials are intentionally flexible and may be adapted to fit the rhythm, size, and pastoral needs of your local church.

Each week of the guide corresponds to a thematic movement in the broader *Bride of Christ* journey. Within each section you will find biblical framing, theological insights, and pastoral reflections intended to assist in sermon preparation, teaching development, and congregational application.

You are not expected to reproduce the material verbatim. Rather, use these resources as pastoral scaffolding – a framework to support your own discernment as you prepare to preach and shepherd your people.

Recommended Ways to Implement the Series

Churches have found several fruitful ways to integrate this material into congregational life. You may choose the approach that best fits your context.

- **Sermon Series**
  Many pastors and ministry leaders use the five movements of *The Bride of Christ* as a focused preaching series. Each week's content is designed to support approximately one week of sermon preparation, though the pacing may be expanded or condensed as desired.

- **Coordinated Churchwide Journey**
  Some congregations choose to align Sunday preaching with small groups using the participant editions of the study. This unified approach often deepens congregational engagement, though it is not required for meaningful impact.

- **Small Group or Formation Emphasis**
  In settings where extended preaching series are not feasible, the themes may be introduced through small groups, seasonal

formation initiatives, or retreat environments, with pastoral teaching woven in as appropriate.

As you prepare to lead each week, many pastors find the following rhythm helpful:

1. Begin with prayerful reading of the week's central theme and Scriptures.
2. Review the theological insights provided in this guide.
3. Discern your pastoral emphasis based on the needs of your congregation.
4. Shape your sermon or teaching in your own voice and context.
5. Encourage deeper engagement through the companion participant resources where appropriate.

The aim is not uniform delivery, but faithful and context-sensitive shepherding.

Other Resources in the Series

This Ministry Guide is part of the broader *Symbol & Silence – Bride of Christ* series. Many churches experience the greatest fruit when the pastoral teaching is paired with the participant materials, which invite individuals and small groups into a more contemplative engagement with Scripture.

At the heart of every resource is the same conviction: the Christian life is not merely information to master, but a relationship to inhabit – a gradual preparation of the people of God for union with Christ.

To support that shared vision, Symbol & Silence offers several companion resources that mirror and extend the experience you encounter in this guide.

Weekly Reflections on Substack

The **Symbol & Silence Substack** offers ongoing narrative reflections that correspond to the movements of the series. These essays are freely available and are designed to prepare the heart, deepen theological imagination, and extend the contemplative posture into daily reading life. Many groups find these reflections helpful as a gentle entry point into each week's theme.

Contemporary Bible Study

For groups that prefer a more discussion-forward format, the **Contemporary Bible Study** edition presents the same theological journey in a structure designed for conversational engagement. While the contemplative guide emphasizes silence and interior noticing, this version provides additional prompts and teaching movement suited to traditional small group settings.

Contemplative Experience

The **Contemplative Experience** invites individuals and small groups into a slower, prayerful engagement with Scripture through silence, breath prayer, and reflective listening. Structured around the same five movements as the broader series, the Contemplative Experience helps participants move beyond information alone into attentive awareness of Christ's presence. It is especially well suited for small groups, retreats, and congregations seeking to deepen the formational impact of the series.

Youth Group Curriculum

Recognizing the importance of forming younger believers, Symbol & Silence also offers a **Youth Group Curriculum** built on the same core themes of belonging, preparation, devotion, hope, and union. The youth materials translate the vision of *The Bride of Christ* into age-appropriate language and interactive experiences for middle school and high school settings.

Together, these resources allow churches and individuals to engage the same spiritual journey across multiple contexts and learning styles. Whether used individually or as a coordinated pathway, the aim remains the same – to help the people of God grow in attentive love, steady hope, and joyful readiness for the life we are being prepared to share with Christ.

A Word of Encouragement

Symbol & Silence rests on the conviction that Scripture is not merely a record of divine speech – it is an invitation into relationship. When approached with prayerful attentiveness, the biblical text becomes a living meeting place between Christ and His people. The imagery of the Divine Bridegroom and His beloved Church is not decorative language, but a window into God's ultimate purpose for those He calls His own.

Your role in this series is the quiet and sacred work of shepherding – helping those entrusted to your care move, step by patient step, toward a more attentive life with Christ. You are not being asked to manufacture outcomes, but to faithfully guide, teach, and trust the steady work of the Spirit. Open the Scriptures, name the movement of God's grace, and create space for the Spirit to work within the life of the church. The One who calls the Church His Bride is already at work among you.

May this guide serve you as you faithfully shepherd those entrusted to your care.

Welcome to the work.

1

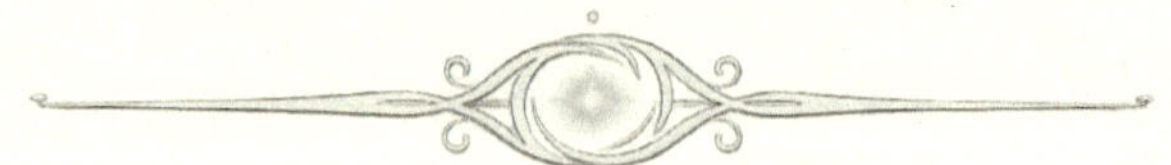

Mystical Union: The Ultimate Hope

Theological Themes & Ministry Connections

Christian hope is often presented as escape from the world, relief from suffering, or the eventual reward of moral living. Yet the marriage imagery of Scripture transports us into a very different story – one in which the ultimate purpose of salvation is union with God.[3] This is not peripheral theology; it is the thread running from the prophets to the apostles, from Israel's unfaithfulness to the Church's glorification.[4]

---

[3] Athanasius, On the Incarnation, trans. John Behr (Yonkers, NY: St. Vladimir's Seminary Press, 2011), 54.
[4] 2 Peter 1:4.

When we speak of mystical union, we are naming the deepest biblical conviction: that humanity was created not merely to obey God, serve God, or imitate God, but to share life with God.

This shifts the pastoral horizon.[5] Discipleship is no longer framed primarily as rule-keeping or self-improvement, but as preparation for relationship. Sanctification becomes a process of beautification – the Bride being made ready. Eschatology becomes relational rather than catastrophic.[6] And the Christian life moves from anxiety to longing, from striving to receiving.

Union also reframes worship. Instead of performing for God, the congregation is invited to be drawn into God's own life. Instead of fearing God's judgment, believers learn to trust God's desire. Instead of imagining heaven as disembodied bliss, the Church begins to anticipate the wedding feast that fulfills the deepest human ache: to be fully known and fully loved.

In ministry contexts, this theme softens hardened hearts, restores the disillusioned, and awakens hope in those who believe God tolerates them but does not desire them.

Union is not merely a reward – it is the goal toward which all redemption moves.

---

[5] See St. Bernard of Clairvaux, On Loving God, trans. Robert Walton (Kalamazoo, MI: Cistercian Publications, 1973).
[6] N. T. Wright, Surprised by Hope (New York: HarperOne, 2008).

Context for Ministry

Modern believers may intellectually affirm that "God loves them"–yet struggle profoundly to experience or trust that love. Many come to church carrying quiet philosophical assumptions formed not by Scripture, but by culture:

1. **A functional deism:**
   Even devout Christians often imagine God as distant–loving in theory, but emotionally detached in practice. They may say, "God is with me," yet feel alone in suffering or abandoned in prayer.

2. **A therapeutic framework:**
   People often approach spirituality primarily for self-help: Will God fix my anxiety? My marriage? My loneliness? Union language can initially feel too lofty until they discover that their deepest ache is not for solutions but for communion.

3. **A moral-performance model of faith:**
   Many assume that God's affection increases or decreases based on their religious success. They live exhausted, subconsciously convinced: If I don't try harder, God will be disappointed. The idea that God longs for them feels too good to believe.

4. **An existential loneliness:**
   Even in community, people feel unseen and unknown. This makes the bridal imagery of Scripture both beautiful and frightening. If God truly desires union, then He sees everything – and that level of intimacy can feel threatening unless it is framed as healing, not scrutiny.

5. **A cultural distrust of intimacy:**
   In a world marked by betrayal, broken relationships, and emotional guardedness, "union with God" can sound like losing oneself or being absorbed into something impersonal. Pastors need to reassure people: divine union does not erase identity – it fulfills it.

6. **A flattened eschatology:**
   For many Christians, hope is either vague ("we go to heaven when we die") or fear-based ("avoid judgment"). Few imagine salvation as relational fulfillment, a wedding, a shared life with God. Clergy must help reawaken a biblical imagination: the Christian hope is not escape, but embrace.

7. **A hunger for more than information:**
   People know far more about God than they know of God. Theological data without relational encounter has left many spiritually numb. Union speaks directly to this ache: the heart longs for presence, not propositions.

Biblical Commentary

- **Old Testament: Hosea 2:14–23 – God's covenantal love portrayed as betrothal.**

  Hosea's prophetic poetry gives Scripture's earliest sustained picture of God as Bridegroom. Here, God does not merely forgive Israel; He woos her. The language is intimate, even vulnerable:

  Expanded Insights:

  - "I will allure her" – God initiates reconciliation not by force but invitation.
  - "I will speak tenderly to her" – divine speech is restorative, not accusatory.
  - "I will betroth you to me forever" – the covenant is framed as a marriage promise renewed, not replaced.

  This text establishes a crucial foundation: union with God is not a New Testament innovation. It is the deep thread woven through Israel's scriptures – God drawing His people into an unbreakable relationship of love.

- **Gospels: John 17:20–26 – Jesus' prayer for oneness and shared life**

  In Jesus' high priestly prayer, we overhear His deepest longing: that humanity would share in the eternal communion of Father and Son.

Expanded Insights:

- "That they may all be one… as You, Father, are in me and I in You" reveals that Christian unity is not mere organizational harmony but participation in divine life.
- "The glory You have given me I have given them" suggests that glory is not prestige but relational fullness – the radiant life of God shared with His people.

Jesus prays this before the crucifixion, reinforcing that the cross is the doorway into communion, not merely the solution to sin.

John 17 grounds union not in human achievement, but in the desire of Christ Himself.

- **Epistles: Ephesians 5:25–32 – The marriage mystery revealed**

  Paul's exhortation to husbands and wives is frequently read as household instruction, but the apostle insists the deeper subject is Christ and the Church. The nuptial imagery is theological before it is ethical.

  Expanded Insights:

  - "Gave himself up for her" draws from temple-sacrifice language; Christ's self-offering is both purifying and deeply relational.

- "That He might present the church to Himself" evokes ancient wedding rituals in which the bridegroom receives the bride adorned and ready.
- "This mystery is profound" signals that marriage does not merely illustrate the gospel – it is woven into the fabric of salvation history.

For Paul, redemption is not the end of the story. The goal is the presentation of the Church to Christ in radiant union.

The Church is being prepared – adorned – for union.

- **Eschatological Vision: Revelation 21:1–5 – The wedding at the end of the age**
  Scripture's final vision is not conquest, not escape, not destruction – but marriage.

  Expanded insights:
  - The New Jerusalem descends "as a bride adorned," echoing Ephesians' language of presentation.
  - "The dwelling place of God is with humanity" shows that the trajectory of redemption is not humanity going up to God, but God coming down to dwell with His people.

The tender acts – wiping tears, removing death – portray union not as an abstract theological event, but a profoundly relational and healing one.

Revelation completes the storyline that began in Hosea and culminated in the prayer of Jesus: God is not content to redeem us from afar; He intends to unite His life with ours forever.

Homiletical & Exegetical Guiding Questions

Textual Questions

- How does Hosea portray God's heart toward unfaithful people?
- What does Jesus pray for most passionately in John 17, and why?
- How does Paul use marriage language to reframe the entire Christian story?
- Why does Revelation end with a wedding rather than a throne?

Theological Questions

- What does it mean that salvation culminates not in deliverance but in union?
- How does a relational eschatology transform our understanding of heaven?
- What implications arise when Christ is portrayed not only as Savior and Lord, but as Bridegroom?

Pastoral Questions

- Where do people in your congregation struggle to believe that God desires them?
- How might the bridal imagery heal shame, fear, or moral exhaustion?
- How does this teaching reframe prayer, discipleship, or suffering?

Formational Questions

- What practices cultivate longing rather than duty?
- What false loves compete with desire for God?
- What does "preparing the Bride" look like in everyday Christian life?

Suggested Sermon Flow

1. **Opening Vision: Recovering the Larger Story**
    a. **Goal:** Surface common assumptions about salvation and gently widen the frame.
    b. You may begin by noting:
        i. Many believers understandably think of salvation primarily in terms of forgiveness.
        ii. Scripture fully affirms this.
        iii. Yet the biblical story consistently moves toward something relational and communal.
    c. **Pastoral tone:** calm, invitational, spacious.

   d. **Optional transition line:** "What if redemption is not only about what we are saved from, but also about what we are being prepared for?"

2. **Human Experience Bridge: The Movement of Love Toward Commitment**
   a. **Goal:** Ground the imagery in familiar human experience without sentimentality.
   b. You might gently observe:
      i. Meaningful relationships tend to move toward deeper commitment.
      ii. When love matures, it often expresses itself publicly and covenantally.
      iii. Throughout history, weddings have marked not merely celebration, but belonging.
   c. You may briefly acknowledge:
      i. Cultural expressions of marriage have changed across time.
      ii. Yet the human longing to be known, chosen, and joined in faithful love remains deeply recognizable.
   d. **Important pastoral note:** Keep the tone observational rather than romanticized, mindful that many listeners carry complex relationship histories.
   e. **Transition:** "This human pattern helps us hear the language Scripture uses when it speaks of Christ and His people."

3. **Scriptural Illumination: The Bride in the Biblical Story**
   a. **Goal:** Let the biblical imagery speak with clarity and weight.

b. Guide the congregation through the chosen text(s), highlighting:
    i. Christ's self-giving love
    ii. the Church being made ready
    iii. Paul's language of mystery
    iv. the wedding imagery in Revelation
    v. Jesus' prayer for shared life in John 17
c. You may briefly note for context: In the first-century world, betrothal and marriage carried profound covenant significance. Preparation for the wedding was understood as a meaningful season of readiness and fidelity.
d. **Important:** Resist over-explaining. Allow the imagery to breathe.

4. **Pastoral Clarification: What Union Does (and Does Not) Mean**
    a. **Goal:** Provide theological safety and clarity.
    b. Gently clarify that union with Christ does **not** mean:
        i. loss of personal identity
        ii. emotional mysticism detached from Scripture
        iii. spiritual elitism
    c. Rather, union speaks of:
        i. shared life with Christ
        ii. faithful belonging
        iii. growing participation in His love
        iv. relational closeness grounded in grace
    d. **Tone:** steady, reassuring, pastorally grounded.
    e. This step is especially helpful for cautious or analytically minded listeners.

5. **Formational Invitation: Living as a People Being Prepared**
    a. **Goal:** Move from doctrine into lived discipleship without pressure.
    b. You might invite the congregation to reflect:
        i. What if the Christian life is a season of preparation for communion?
        ii. Where might Christ already be quietly forming us?
        iii. How might this vision reshape our ordinary faithfulness?
    c. Encourage the congregation this week to:
        i. notice Christ's patient work
        ii. remain attentive in small acts of faithfulness
        iii. receive formation as grace rather than striving
        iv. **Important:** Frame this as invitation, not demand.

6. **Closing Image: The Joy Set Before the Church**
    a. **Goal:** Leave the congregation with hope-filled imagination.
    b. You may return to the wedding imagery of Revelation and remind the congregation:
        i. Christ is not merely rescuing a people. He is preparing a people.
        ii. And the story is moving toward joy.
    c. **Optional closing line:** "The story of redemption is moving somewhere beautiful — and by His grace, we are being prepared for it."

7. **Bridge to the Next Week**
    a. You may close by noting:

i. If the Church is being prepared as a Bride, the natural next question becomes: How does that preparation actually unfold in the life of believers?
ii. (This prepares the congregation naturally for **Getting Ready for the Big Day**.)

Pastoral Emphases for the Week

Leaders may wish to emphasize:

- salvation as relational and covenantal
- Christ's initiative in forming His people
- the dignity and destiny of the Church
- hope that steadies ordinary discipleship
- formation as patient, grace-filled work

Potential Challenges to Address Gently

Some listeners may:

- be unfamiliar with bridal theology
- carry complicated marriage experiences
- default to purely transactional views of salvation
- feel cautious about mystical language

Address these by:

- staying anchored in Scripture
- keeping the tone pastoral
- emphasizing historic Christian continuity
- avoiding speculative language

2

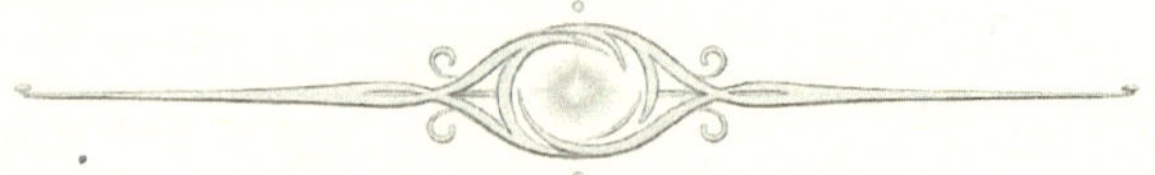

Getting Ready for the Big Day

Theological Themes and Ministry Connections

Christian tradition has long held that salvation is not merely an act but a transformation – not simply a gift received, but a life continually reshaped into the likeness of Christ.[7] This week's theme centers on that lifelong preparation. Scripture describes the Church as a Bride being made ready, not through anxious striving or moral self-improvement, but through the slow and steady work of communion. Formation is relational before it is ethical.[8] It arises from abiding rather than performing.

Isaiah's vision of the Bride clothed in garments of salvation gives the first glimpse of this truth: readiness begins with God's initiative. He dresses

---

[7] 2 Corinthians 3:17–18; Philippians 1:6.

[8] Dallas Willard, Renovation of the Heart (Colorado Springs: NavPress, 2002).

His people in righteousness that they themselves could not weave. Jesus extends this imagery through the metaphor of the vine and branches – a reminder that fruit does not come from effort but from nearness. To abide is to allow Christ's life to flow into our own, shaping us from the inside out.

Paul then articulates the interior movement beneath these images. As believers "behold the Lord's glory," the Spirit transforms them step by step into the image of Christ. Formation, in this sense, is not the improvement of the will but the unification of the will – a deepening alignment between God's desires and our own. The ego slowly loosens its grip as the soul turns outward in love.

Revelation provides the horizon toward which all this preparation points: the wedding feast of the Lamb. The Bride "makes herself ready," yet her readiness is described as something "granted" by God. This paradox is central to Christian spirituality: the Bride participates in her preparation, yet the very capacity to desire, to change, and to love comes from the One who loves her. Formation is grace in motion.

For ministry, these themes touch the heart of discipleship. Many congregants believe they must transform themselves before approaching God, or that spiritual growth is measured by accomplishments rather than surrender. This week offers a counter-narrative: the Christian life is not self-improvement – it is participation in divine life. Leaders can help their communities see formation as a joyful process of becoming, grounded in hope and sustained by God's initiative.

Week 2 invites pastors and ministry leaders to consider how their ministries cultivate environments where people can *abide*. Programs and teaching have their place, but transformation ultimately springs from encounter: prayer that opens the heart, worship that lifts the eyes, fellowship that reflects Christ's character, silence that forms receptivity. The task of spiritual leadership is not to produce holiness but to create space where holiness can take root.

In every generation, the Church wrestles with the tension between doing and becoming. This week's focus returns us to the center: we become the Bride by staying close to the Bridegroom. Formation is not a burden to bear but a promise to receive. The Church that understands this will not only prepare well – it will flourish in hope, joy, and love.

Context for Ministry

Modern Christians are exhausted by self-improvement. Many believers assume spiritual growth is a religious version of self-optimization: trying harder, behaving better, appearing more "together." Beneath this lies fear – fear of falling short, fear of disappointing God, fear of never being enough. This exhaustion becomes the silent backdrop to their spiritual lives.

1. **Most people confuse sanctification with performance:**
   When Scripture speaks of "making ourselves ready," many hear a demand for flawless behavior. They imagine God waiting for them to become worthy rather than shaping them through grace. The Christian life becomes pressure rather than preparation.

2. **Our culture reinforces the idea that transformation is self-generated:**
   We live in an era dominated by personal branding, self-curation, and psychological self-improvement. Even in the church, this worldview creeps in. People think they must engineer their own spiritual maturity – as though holiness were a project they must manage.

3. **Biblical preparation is not self-improvement; it is participation:**
   Scripture consistently portrays transformation as something God initiates and we receive. "We are being transformed… by the Spirit" (2 Cor. 3:18). Growth is relational, not mechanical.[9] It is the Bride being shaped by the love of the Bridegroom.

4. **Sanctification is the slow death of ego and the rising of love:**
   Growth in Christ does not begin with moral upgrading but with surrender: releasing control, shedding self-justification, and

[9] Andrew Murray, Abide in Christ (1882; repr., Uhrichsville, OH: Barbour, 2002).

allowing love to reorder our motivations. We prepare for Christ not by becoming impressive, but by becoming available.

5. **Preparation is a sign of longing, not legalism:**
   In ancient Jewish betrothal, the bride prepared because she desired union – her readiness was an act of love. Likewise, Christian formation flows from desire, not duty. The more fully we long for Christ, the more naturally we open to His shaping.

6. **Believers need help imagining sanctification as joy, not pressure:**
   Many have only known transformation as a demand. Week 2 invites them to see it as gift: the Spirit sculpting them into someone who can enjoy God forever. This reframes the Christian life, not as a test to pass but as a wedding to anticipate.

Biblical Commentary

- **Old Testament: Isaiah 61:10–11 – The Clothing of Righteousness as Bridal Preparation**
  Isaiah envisions salvation through the imagery of adornment: God clothes His people as a bride prepared for her wedding: *"He has clothed me with garments of salvation… as a bride adorns herself with her jewels."*

This imagery is not cosmetic; it is covenantal. In Israelite culture, wedding garments symbolized readiness, dignity, and relational belonging. Isaiah uses this metaphor to show that God Himself provides what His people cannot manufacture – their beauty, righteousness, and readiness.

Expanded Insights:

- The text also emphasizes divine initiative: *"The Sovereign Lord will make righteousness and praise spring up before all nations."*

Preparation is pictured less as human effort and more as God causing His people to become what they were meant to be.

Isaiah establishes the foundational truth: God prepares His Bride by clothing her in His own righteousness.

- **Gospels: John 15:1–5 – Abiding as the Process of Becoming Like Christ**

  Jesus offers His disciples not a method of self-improvement, but a metaphor of dependence: *"I am the vine; you are the branches."*

Fruitfulness does not come from striving, but from connection. The verb "abide" (μένω) implies staying, dwelling, remaining in communion.

Expanded insights:

- Formation is organic, not mechanical.
- Growth is relational before it is behavioral.
- The source of transformation is Christ's life flowing into ours.

The pruning imagery speaks directly to Week 2's theme: God removes what does not belong, not to punish, but to make room for greater fruitfulness.

This text reframes spiritual preparation: instead of "improving ourselves," we are learning to stay where grace can reach us.

Epistles: 2 Corinthians 3:17–18 – Being Transformed by the Spirit

Paul describes the Christian life as a gradual unveiling: *"We are being transformed into his image with ever-increasing glory… which comes from the Lord, who is the Spirit."*

Expanded Insights:

- **Passive voice** – "we are being transformed," God's doing the work in us.
- **Present tense** – transformation is ongoing, not instantaneous.
- **Into His image** – the goal of preparation is nothing less than Christlikeness.

For Paul, spiritual transformation is not self-engineered. It is a relational dynamic: the Spirit shapes us as we behold Christ. This directly supports the theme of "making ourselves ready" not through pressure or fear, but through participation in a divine process already underway.

- **Eschatological Vision: Revelation 19:6–8 – The Bride Made Ready**
  Revelation's great wedding image gives ultimate context to Christian formation: *"The wedding of the Lamb has come, and His Bride has made herself ready."*

Expanded Insights:

  - Notice the beautiful paradox:
  - "It was granted her to clothe herself." – God's grace provides.
  - "with fine linen, bright and pure, for the fine linen is the righteous deeds of the saints." – the Bride participates.

Here, preparation is both gift and response. Everything the Bride offers originates in God's generosity, yet her readiness is expressed through real change, real faithfulness, real action.

Revelation shows the end toward which all formation bends: the presentation of a people fully prepared for union.

This is not a peripheral motif. It is the Bible's vision of Christian hope. Formation is bridal, relational, and eschatological.

Homiletical and Exegetical Questions

Textual Questions

- What does Isaiah's imagery of "garments of salvation" reveal about who prepares the Bride?
- How does John 15 redefine spiritual growth – what does Jesus emphasize, and what does He omit?
- In 2 Corinthians 3, what does it mean that "we are being transformed" rather than transforming ourselves?
- How does Revelation 19 hold together both divine initiative and human participation in preparation?

Theological Questions

- What does Scripture suggest is the true aim of formation: improvement or union?
- How does the interplay of grace and participation shape our understanding of sanctification?
- What does it mean that Christian transformation is relational rather than mechanical?
- How does bridal imagery reshape our understanding of holiness?

Pastoral Questions

- Where do people confuse spiritual preparation with pressure or perfectionism?
- How might the metaphor of abiding relieve the fear of "not doing enough"?
- Where do you see believers striving rather than receiving what God provides?
- How can you help your people imagine spiritual growth as a joyful preparation rather than a burden?

Formational Questions

- What practices help your community abide rather than achieve?
- How might your church create space for God to form people rather than expecting them to self-form?
- What "false preparation" (self-improvement, appearances, performance) needs to be named and released?
- What signs of genuine transformation, however small, can your people learn to recognize and celebrate?

Suggested Sermon Flow

1. **Opening Vision: The Meaningful Work of Preparation**
    a. **Goal:** Surface the familiar human experience of getting ready for something that matters.
    b. You may begin by observing:

        i. When something meaningful approaches, people naturally begin to prepare.
        ii. Important moments have a way of reshaping our attention and priorities.
        iii. Preparation often reveals what we value most.
    c. Gently introduce the spiritual parallel:
        i. Scripture speaks of the people of God as living in a season of preparation — not merely waiting for the future, but being quietly formed for it.
    d. **Tone:** calm, invitational, hope-filled.
    e. **Optional transition line:** "Throughout the New Testament, the Church is described as a Bride being made ready."

2. **Human Experience Bridge: Readiness as Orientation of the Heart**
    a. **Goal:** Ground the theme in recognizable relational experience.
    b. You might gently note:
        i. In the ancient world, the season before a wedding was marked by intentional readiness.
        ii. A bride's preparation was not primarily about outward arrangements, but about readiness of life and fidelity of heart.
        iii. The preparation itself expressed where love was directed.
    c. You may briefly acknowledge:

    i. Cultural expressions of marriage have changed over time.
    ii. Yet the human experience of preparing for meaningful commitment remains widely understood.

d. **Pastoral sensitivity:** Keep language spacious and inclusive, mindful of varied relationship histories.
e. **Transition:** "This background helps us hear the depth of the imagery Scripture uses for the people of God."

3. **Scriptural Illumination: The Bride Who Makes Herself Ready**
    a. **Goal:** Let the biblical text carry the theological weight.
    b. Guide the congregation through the primary passage(s), highlighting:
        i. Revelation's declaration: *"the Bride has made herself ready"*
        ii. Paul's concern to present the Church in faithful devotion
        iii. the Psalm's imagery of attentive turning toward the King
    c. Key themes to surface:
        i. readiness as grace-enabled
        ii. preparation as relational
        iii. formation as patient and ongoing
        iv. love as the motivating center

   d. **Important:** Avoid framing readiness as self-driven spiritual improvement. Let the imagery breathe.

4. **Pastoral Clarification: Preparation Is Not Religious Pressure**
   a. **Goal:** Remove common misunderstandings that may arise.
   b. Gently clarify that biblical preparation is **not**:
      i. Perfectionism
      ii. anxious striving
      iii. earning God's approval
      iv. spiritual performance
   c. Rather, readiness describes:
      i. a heart gradually being reordered
      ii. affections learning to turn toward Christ
      iii. habits being gently reshaped over time
      iv. love becoming more focused and steady
   d. **Tone:** reassuring, freeing, grace-centered.

5. **Formational Invitation: Ordering the Affections**
   a. **Goal:** Offer concrete but gentle life application.
   b. You may invite the congregation to reflect this week:
      i. What in my life draws me toward deeper love for Christ?
      ii. What quietly fragments or distracts my attention?
      iii. Where might the Spirit already be inviting gentle reordering?

c. Encourage simple responses such as:
    i. renewed attentiveness in prayer
    ii. simplifying unnecessary distractions
    iii. small acts of faithful obedience
    iv. quiet responsiveness to Christ's presence
d. **Important:** Frame all movement as response to grace, not self-effort.

6. **Closing Image: The Quiet Beauty of Readiness**
    a. **Goal:** Leave the congregation with hope-filled imagination.
    b. Return to Revelation's vision of the Bride.
    c. Emphasize:
        i. The Bride is not hurried.
        ii. She is not anxious.
        iii. She is being made ready.
    d. Reassure the congregation:
        i. Christ is faithful to complete what He begins.
        ii. The work of preparation is itself evidence of His love.
    e. **Optional closing line:** "The One who calls His people is also the One who patiently prepares them."

7. **Bridge to the Next Week**
    a. As the heart becomes more steadily oriented toward Christ, another question naturally emerges: What must we release so that our love may become undivided?

3

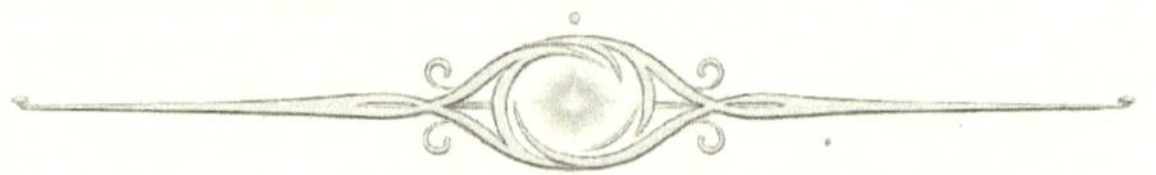

Forsaking All Others

Theological Themes & Ministry Connections

To speak of "forsaking all others" is not to romanticize asceticism nor to shame human longing. Scripture consistently treats desire as a profound spiritual force – one that can be beautifully ordered or disastrously misdirected.[10] The human heart does not stop loving when it turns toward lesser things; it simply loves poorly. This week's theme invites clergy and congregants alike into the deeper work of discerning the desires that compete with God for allegiance.

At the center of this theme is the biblical revelation that God is the initiator of covenant love. Hosea shows us a God who binds Himself to

---

[10] St. Augustine, Confessions, trans. Henry Chadwick (Oxford: Oxford University Press, 1991), I.1

an unfaithful people, not because of their devotion but because of His. Preaching this theme requires careful pastoral nuance: God does not demand fidelity before offering His own; His fidelity *creates* the possibility of ours. This reorients the congregation – forsaking is not legalism, but liberation.

Jesus' teaching on divided allegiance gives ministers a practical lens into contemporary idolatry. In modern life, rival "masters" rarely appear as carved images; they emerge as cultural scripts – achievement, security, self-sufficiency, identity-making. Pastors can help people identify the subtle ways these narratives shape their loyalties. Jesus does not condemn possessions or responsibilities; He names the way they threaten to become ultimate. Ministers can shepherd congregants to ask: *What do I look to for meaning, safety, or worth?* Wherever the answer is not God, a competing devotion is revealed.

James offers another dimension: loyalty is not only theological but relational. When desire aligns with envy, rivalry, or self-promotion, the community fractures. A sermon on this passage may focus on how divided desire harms the body of Christ – and how fidelity to God naturally fosters fidelity to one another. Pastors can explore practical examples: office competition, family conflicts, ministry territorialism, church politics. These are not merely interpersonal issues; they are symptoms of a heart divided.

Revelation provides the eschatological horizon: the Bride being made ready. Here, pastoral teaching can help congregants imagine the Christian life not as moral tightening but as bridal preparation – the beautification of the soul through love. Many people understand sanctification as rule-keeping or sin-management. This passage reframes it as adornment. Ministers might ask their people: *What am I wearing before the Lord? What garments of love, mercy, and purity is He weaving into my life?*

Week 3 therefore calls clergy to guide their people into the holy work of reordering their desires. Forsaking all others is not a withdrawal from life but a reorientation within it – choosing a singular love that brings clarity, freedom, and wholeness. In preaching, teaching, or small groups, leaders can help people name the "other loves" that pull at their hearts and gently invite them to turn toward the One who alone satisfies.

Context For Ministry

1. **The modern world is saturated with rival loves:**
   People are not choosing between God and nothing; they are choosing between God and a thousand alluring alternatives – success, security, affirmation, identity, comfort, control. Each one promises meaning and forms the heart in ways that compete with divine love.

2. **We live in an age that prizes autonomy as the highest virtue:**
   To "forsake all others" sounds threatening in a culture that equates freedom with limitless choice. Many assume that

commitment restricts the self, rather than completes it. This makes covenantal devotion feel foreign, even suspicious.

3. **Fear and duty often masquerade as love in the spiritual life.** Many believers were formed to obey God primarily out of fear of consequences or out of obligation. Both fear and duty can produce compliance, but neither produces intimacy. Pastors must help people recognize these motivations without shame – and invite them into the freedom of love.

4. **Desire itself is contested territory.** People are taught to distrust desire, repress it, indulge it, or ignore it. Few are taught to *offer* desire to God or allow Him to shape it. But biblical faith does not eliminate desire – it purifies and redirects it.

5. **We live in a performance-driven culture that misunderstands holiness.** Most Christians assume that "forsaking all others" means stricter rule-keeping or behavior modification. But Scripture frames holiness as fidelity – the turning of the heart toward the One who loves us. Ministers must gently redirect people away from moralism and toward relational transformation.

6. **Spiritual formation requires naming false loves with compassion.**
   People are rarely aware of what truly drives them – approval, fear, scarcity, ambition, image, belonging. The task is not condemnation but clarity. When these "other loves" are spoken aloud, they lose their power to hide in the shadows.[11]

7. **The heart is shaped by what it loves most.**
   This week invites the community to examine the attachments that silently shape their decisions, habits, and affections. Forsaking all others is not about loss; it is about becoming free enough to love God creatively, wholeheartedly, and joyfully.

Biblical Commentary

Forsaking all others is not a command to tighten our grip, but an invitation to *loosen* the attachments that dilute our love. Scripture portrays God as the faithful Bridegroom whose unwavering devotion awakens ours. Jesus calls us to clarity about the masters we serve. James urges us to draw near with undivided affection. Revelation shows the end toward which all devotion moves – a Bride made ready through the purification of love.

---

[11] Augustine, Confessions, XIII; see also Thomas Aquinas, Summa Theologiae, I–II, q. 84.

To forsake all others is not to shrink life but to open ourselves to the single love that transforms every other love.

- **Old Testament: Hosea 2:19–20 – God's Covenant Fidelity**
  Hosea stands as one of Scripture's clearest portrayals of covenant fidelity in the face of infidelity. Israel's unfaithfulness is not treated merely as disobedience but as adultery of the heart – the turning of affection toward competing lovers. Yet God responds not with rejection but with a renewed vow. These verses reveal the surprising tenderness of God's covenant love: He binds Himself to a people who have repeatedly abandoned Him. Here the theme of forsaking all others begins not with human effort but divine commitment – God's unwavering fidelity becomes the ground of our own.

- **Gospel: Matthew 6:24 – Undivided Allegiance**
  Jesus does not treat divided loyalty as a minor spiritual inconvenience; He presents it as an impossibility. The human heart will always attach itself somewhere – and wherever it attaches, it will serve. In this teaching, Jesus exposes how subtle "other loves" become functional masters: security, wealth, approval, self-sufficiency. His words invite us to clarity: discipleship is not merely adding God to our priorities but offering Him exclusive allegiance. Forsaking all others is not renouncing earthly goods; it is refusing to make them ultimate.

- **Epistle: James 4:4–8 – Turning from Rival Loves**
  James speaks with pastoral urgency about misplaced affections. "Friendship with the world" does not mean rejecting creation but rejecting the world's value system – ambition rooted in envy, identity rooted in status, desire rooted in self-exaltation. These rival loves fracture the soul. Yet James offers a path toward restoration: *Draw near.* Devotion begins not with perfection but direction – turning toward God with a sincere heart. Forsaking all others is fundamentally about **reorientation**, not moral performance.

- **Eschatological Vision: Revelation 19:7–8 – The Bride Made Ready**
  At the culmination of Scripture's story stands a wedding – the fulfillment of divine union toward which all covenant love points. The Bride "makes herself ready," not through self-generated purity, but by receiving the radiant garments given to her. This eschatological vision reframes Christian devotion as preparation for union. Every act of fidelity, every surrender of rival loves, every movement toward wholehearted affection becomes part of the Bride's readiness. Forsaking all others is not ascetic loss but bridal becoming – a joyful alignment with love's final horizon.

Homiletical and Exegetical Questions

Textual Questions

- What does Hosea 2 reveal about God's posture toward an unfaithful people?
- How does Jesus' teaching in Matthew 6:24 expose the nature of divided allegiance?
- What does James mean by "friendship with the world," and how does he connect it to the heart's desires?
- How does Revelation's bridal imagery reframe fidelity as preparation for union?

Theological Questions

- What does Scripture suggest is the true nature of idolatry – behavior or desire?
- How does God's covenant fidelity shape our understanding of human fidelity?
- What distinguishes fear-based obedience, duty-based obedience, and love-based obedience?
- How does forsaking rival loves make room for deeper communion with God?

Pastoral Questions

- Where do people experience divided loyalty without realizing it?
- Which "other loves" most commonly compete with affection for God – approval, security, success, identity, comfort?
- How might fear or duty be masquerading as devotion in the lives of your people?
- What gentle pathways can help congregants name and release attachments without shame?

Formational Questions

- What practices help the community discern desire – noticing what the heart clings to and why?
- How can you guide people toward offering their desires to God instead of suppressing or indulging them?
- What small acts of fidelity might help the congregation turn toward God with greater freedom?
- What would it look like for your community to become a people of "unmixed love"?

Suggested Sermon Flow

1. **Opening Vision: Love Naturally Seeks Wholeness**
    a. **Goal:** Surface a familiar human truth about devotion.
    b. You may begin by observing:
        i. Deep love has a way of clarifying our priorities.

        ii. When something (or someone) matters deeply, competing loyalties begin to feel more noticeable.
        iii. This is not usually experienced as restriction, but as the natural movement of devotion.
    c. Gently connect:
        i. Scripture suggests that the same dynamic unfolds in the life of faith. As love for God matures, the heart itself begins to simplify.
    d. **Tone:** calm, understanding, non-accusatory.
    e. **Optional transition line:** "The Bible sometimes describes this movement with a striking phrase: forsaking all others."

2. **Human Experience Bridge: The Language of Faithful Love**
    a. **Goal:** Ground the phrase in relational reality.
    b. You might gently note:
        i. In covenant relationships, exclusivity is not primarily about loss but about belonging.
        ii. To pledge fidelity has historically meant directing one's deepest loyalty toward one beloved.
        iii. The language may sound strong, but its purpose is relational clarity, not emotional severity.
    c. You may briefly acknowledge:
        i. Modern listeners may hear such language differently than first-century audiences.
        ii. Yet the human longing for faithful, undivided love remains deeply familiar.

d. **Pastoral sensitivity:** Avoid romantic idealization; keep tone spacious and humane.
e. **Transition:** "This helps us hear the depth of the invitation Scripture is making."

3. **Scriptural Illumination: Drawing Near with an Undivided Heart**
   a. **Goal:** Let the biblical texts speak clearly and gently.
   b. Guide the congregation through the primary passages, highlighting:
      i. James's invitation to draw near to God
      ii. Hosea's language of faithful covenant love
      iii. Mary's attentive posture at Jesus' feet
   c. Key themes to surface:
      i. God's initiating love
      ii. the invitation to nearness
      iii. the quiet exposure of divided attention
      iv. devotion as relational response
   d. **Important:** Emphasize that Scripture's tone is invitational before it is corrective. Let the texts breathe.

4. **Pastoral Clarification: This Is Not About Harsh Renunciation**
   a. **Goal:** Remove common fears and misinterpretations.
   b. Gently clarify that "forsaking all others" does **not** mean:
      i. abandoning healthy relationships
      ii. withdrawing from ordinary responsibilities

iii. adopting rigid asceticism
iv. striving to prove devotion
c. Rather, it describes:
i. the heart's growing freedom
ii. love becoming more focused
iii. misplaced dependencies loosening
iv. Christ becoming more central over time
d. **Tone:** deeply reassuring and freeing. This is the most pastorally sensitive moment of the week.

5. **Formational Invitation: Noticing What Holds Our Attention**
a. **Goal:** Offer gentle, non-pressured life application.
b. You may invite the congregation this week to notice:
i. What most consistently captures my emotional energy?
ii. Where do I instinctively look for security or identity?
iii. Where might Christ be inviting quiet re-centering?
c. Encourage simple practices such as:
i. brief moments of attentive prayer
ii. releasing unnecessary inner noise
iii. small acts of trust
iv. returning attention to Christ throughout the day
d. **Important:** Frame this as gentle awareness, not spiritual self-scrutiny.

6. **Closing Image: The Freedom of an Undivided Heart**

a. **Goal:** Leave the congregation with hope, not heaviness. You may return to the bridal imagery and emphasize: God's desire is not to narrow our lives, but to free our love.
b. As the heart becomes less divided:
    i. peace deepens
    ii. clarity grows
    iii. joy becomes more stable
    iv. communion becomes more natural
c. **Optional closing line:** "What God gently removes, He removes to make room for greater love."

7. **Bridge to the Next Week**
    a. You may conclude by noting: As the heart becomes more firmly anchored in Christ, we begin to discover a steadier hope, even in a world that remains deeply broken.

4

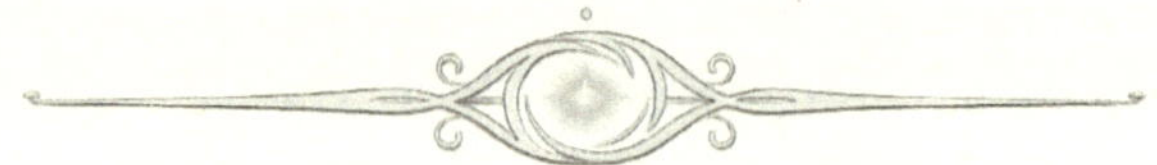

Hope in the Midst of a Broken World

Theological Themes & Ministry Connections

Christian hope is often misunderstood. Many congregants imagine hope as optimism, positive thinking, or emotional uplift. Others see it as naïve – a fragile posture easily broken by the harshness of the world. Scripture, however, presents something very different: a hope rooted not in circumstances but in communion.

Across this week's texts, we encounter a hope that is not passive resignation nor frantic striving. It is a hope that *abides* – a relational posture of remaining in Christ while the world remains unfinished.[12] Abiding holds longing and trust together without collapsing one into the other.

Isaiah's prophetic promise reframes hope as *renewed strength* for a people who feel forgotten. John's Gospel places that renewal in the context of union with Christ: hope grows where communion deepens. Paul, writing to the Romans, names the ache of waiting – not as failure, but as the very form hope takes in a world still being redeemed. And Revelation widens the horizon further: Christian hope always reaches beyond the visible, anchoring itself in God's final act of restoration.

For ministry, these themes converge in a crucial insight:

> **People are not losing hope because they lack information. They are losing hope because they are disconnected from the Source of life.**

Abiding becomes the bridge between theological truth and lived experience.

Clergy will encounter parishioners who are exhausted, disillusioned, grieving, or overwhelmed by global and personal brokenness. These texts teach us that the pastoral task is not to offer quick fixes or emotional

---

[12] Jürgen Moltmann, The Coming of God (Minneapolis: Fortress Press, 1996).

Band-Aids. Rather, it is to shepherd people into staying close to Christ, where hope is not forced but formed.[13]

Abiding becomes a practical spirituality:

- When the world feels chaotic, abiding is the discipline of remaining.
- When the heart feels weak, abiding is the practice of drawing strength from God.
- When suffering obscures meaning, abiding is the courage to wait with God, not apart from Him.
- When lesser hopes fail, abiding reorients the soul toward the hope that does not disappoint.

Ministry rooted in these themes leads congregations away from escapism and into endurance, not by willpower but by union. It helps people see that hope is not an event; it is a relationship. And in that relationship, the church becomes a sign of the coming kingdom – a community marked by patience, resilience, and quiet confidence in the God who will make all things new.

Context for Ministry

To help leaders guide their communities into a hope that does not deny sorrow, but refuses to be defined by it – a hope rooted not in changing

[13] Dietrich Bonhoeffer, Letters and Papers from Prison (New York: Touchstone, 1997)

circumstances, but in the unchanging presence of the One who abides with us.

1. **Modern people are exhausted by hoping in things that cannot hold the weight of their longing.**
   For many, hope is little more than optimism; a fragile belief that circumstances will improve if we wait long enough or work hard enough. Others turn hope into sentimentality, a vague wish that life might "get better someday." And still others have abandoned hope altogether, deciding that realism means expecting nothing so they cannot be disappointed.

2. **Scripture presents a different vision entirely.**
   Biblical hope is not optimism, and it is not denial. It is not rooted in probability, personality, or willpower. It is rooted in a Person – the God who has entered history, who has spoken promises, and who will bring those promises to completion.

3. **Abiding, then, becomes the posture of Christian hope.**
   It is not passive waiting, as though God were distant, nor frantic striving, as though everything depended on us. Abiding is the sustained, steady orientation of a soul anchored in God's future while living faithfully in the present. It is the kind of hope that looks honestly at the world's brokenness and still whispers, "Come, Lord Jesus," not out of despair, but out of trust.

4. **People today are wrestling with a crisis of delay.**
   They wait for healing that has not come, relationships that remain strained, injustices that persist, and prayers that seem unanswered. Many wonder: *How long, O Lord?* This week speaks into that ache – not to resolve it, but to accompany it with a greater promise.

5. **The Christian life holds tension: we live between what is and what will be.**
   Abiding hope teaches us how to inhabit that space without losing heart. It teaches us how to hold longing without cynicism, how to hold grief without collapse, how to hold joy without presumption. It anchors us in the truth that God's future is already breaking into the present.

Biblical Commentary

- **Old Testament: Isaiah 40:27–31 – Strength for the weary; hope that is renewed, not manufactured.**
  Isaiah speaks to a people who feel forgotten by God and overwhelmed by their circumstances – a community convinced that God "does not see" and "does not know." Into this despair, the prophet offers a vision of divine faithfulness that transcends human exhaustion. Hope here is not an emotional high or a temporary burst of optimism; it is participation in God's sustaining life. "Those who wait for the Lord shall renew their

strength" suggests a hope that is received rather than produced. This text frames biblical hope as abiding trust in God's character even when evidence seems scarce.

- **Gospel: John 15:4–11 – Abiding as the central posture of discipleship.**
  Jesus' image of the vine and branches provides the clearest biblical picture of what it means to abide. Hope is not peripheral; it flows from remaining in Him. The disciple does not strive toward God, nor drift away to self-reliance. Rather, the disciple's life is sustained by continual, relational closeness to Christ. Abiding is not passive. It is an intentional orientation – a settled willingness to stay, to remain, to draw life from a source beyond oneself. When read alongside Isaiah 40, this passage shows that renewed strength and enduring hope are fruits of deep communion, not spiritual performance.

- **Epistle: Romans 8:18–25 – Hope grounded in God's future, held in present suffering.**
  Paul situates Christian hope within the vast story of creation's redemption. The world is groaning, the Spirit is groaning, and we ourselves groan – yet this groaning is labor pain, not death throes. Hope here is eschatological: it looks beyond the visible and anchors itself in the promised renewal of all things. Paul insists that hope requires patience, not because God is slow, but because we live between the "already" and the "not yet" of

redemption. This text helps communities understand that longing and ache are not signs of weak faith; they are signs that our hope is aimed toward something real.

- **Eschatological Vision: Revelation 21:1–5 – The hope we await, that God is making all things new.**
  Revelation gives shape to Christian longing. The end of the story is not escape from the world but the renewal of it. God dwells with His people, tears are wiped away, and death is no more. This vision reframes all lesser hopes and protects the church from shrinking hope into personal success or political victories. Revelation 21 reminds the community that abiding is not vague. optimism but anticipation of the God who will finish what He has begun. This is hope that holds steady in brokenness because it is anchored in a future that God Himself guarantees.

Homiletical and Exegetical Questions

Textual Questions

- What is Isaiah contrasting when he speaks of those who "grow weary" versus those who "wait for the Lord"?
- In John 15, how does Jesus define the relationship between "remaining" and "fruit-bearing"?
- In Romans 8, what is the significance of the whole creation "groaning" alongside the children of God?

- How does Revelation's image of God dwelling with humanity reshape our understanding of hope?
- What verbs or images repeat across these passages, and what might those repetitions reveal about Christian endurance?

Theological Questions

- What distinguishes Christian hope from optimism, moral resolve, or wishful thinking?
- How does the biblical idea of *remaining in Christ* challenge the assumption that hope depends on external outcomes?
- Why is the experience of longing, groaning, or waiting described as essential rather than problematic in Christian spirituality?
- How does eschatology (the final restoration of all things) ground hope in something more stable than present circumstances?
- What does it mean that hope is formed not by escape from suffering, but by abiding in God through it?

Pastoral Questions

- Where are people in your congregation likely to feel worn down, weary, or near the limits of resilience?
- How might a sermon on abiding offer comfort without slipping into passivity, or challenge without promoting striving?
- How can you help people differentiate between temporary hopes (career, health, stability) and the ultimate hope that anchors the soul?

- What practices of presence (silence, breath prayer, stillness, community) might help parishioners reconnect to the Source of hope?
- How can you preach hope in a way that is honest about brokenness yet unwavering in the promise of God's future?

Formational Questions

- How is the Spirit inviting your congregation to "remain" with Christ rather than rush toward solutions?
- Where might God be calling individuals or communities to wait with Him, not merely wait for change?
- What small acts of endurance, constancy, or gentle trust could form your people into a hopeful community?
- How might abiding shift how your congregation shows up in relationships, work, conflict, or suffering?
- What would it look like for your church to become a place where people learn not just to believe in hope, but to *practice* hope?

Suggested Sermon Flow

1. **Opening Vision: The Reality of Living Between Promise and Pain**
   a. **Goal:** Name the shared human experience of tension and waiting.

b. You may begin by observing:
   i. Much of life is lived in the space between what we hope for and what we currently see.
   ii. Faith does not remove us from a broken world.
   iii. Even faithful believers experience uncertainty, disappointment, and longing.

c. Gently connect: Scripture speaks honestly about this tension and offers a kind of hope that does not depend on immediate resolution.

d. **Tone:** calm, empathetic, deeply pastoral.

e. **Optional transition line:** "The people of God have always learned to live with hope in the middle of an unfinished story."

2. **Human Experience Bridge: The Kind of Hope That Endures**

   a. **Goal:** Ground the concept of hope in lived experience.

   b. You might gently note:
      i. There is a difference between optimism and hope.
      ii. Optimism depends on favorable outcomes.
      iii. Hope, at its deepest level, is rooted in trust, especially trust in a faithful person.

   c. You may observe:
      i. In strong relationships, trust allows people to remain steady even when circumstances are uncertain.

ii. Scripture invites believers into this deeper, relational kind of hope.

d. **Pastoral sensitivity:** Avoid minimizing real suffering; keep tone compassionate and grounded.

e. **Transition:** "This is the kind of hope the New Testament consistently describes."

3. **Scriptural Illumination: Holding Fast in the In-Between**

   a. **Goal:** Let the biblical texts anchor the message.

   b. Guide the congregation through the passages, highlighting:

      i. Paul's language of present suffering and future glory (Romans 8)

      ii. Jesus' honest promise of trouble alongside His gift of peace (John 16)

      iii. the call to hold fast because God is faithful (Hebrews 10)

   c. Key themes to surface:

      i. honest realism about the world

      ii. future-oriented hope

      iii. Christ's sustaining presence

      iv. faithfulness as the ground of confidence

   d. **Important:** Let Scripture carry emotional weight; avoid over-explanation.

4. **Pastoral Clarification: Hope Is Not Denial**

   a. **Goal:** Remove common misunderstandings.

b. Gently clarify that Christian hope is **not**:
   i. pretending everything is fine
   ii. suppressing grief or struggle
   iii. forced positivity
   iv. spiritual avoidance of pain
c. Rather, biblical hope is:
   i. clear-eyed about the present
   ii. anchored in Christ's faithfulness
   iii. patient in the waiting
   iv. steady in uncertainty
d. **Tone:** deeply reassuring and emotionally intelligent.

5. **Formational Invitation: Practicing Steady Faithfulness**
   a. **Goal:** Offer grounded life application.
   b. You may invite the congregation this week to consider:
      i. Where am I being invited to remain steady rather than reactive?
      ii. What would it look like to practice quiet trust in this season?
      iii. How might I hold fast to Christ in small, ordinary ways?
   c. Encourage simple practices such as:
      i. honest prayer in difficult moments
      ii. returning attention to Christ during anxiety
      iii. small acts of faithfulness in daily life
      iv. patient endurance without self-pressure
   d. **Important:** Keep the invitation gentle and realistic.

6. **Closing Image — The Bride Who Waits in Hope**
    a. **Goal:** Leave the congregation with calm confidence.
    b. Return to the bridal imagery:
        i. The Bride is still waiting.
        ii. The world is still unfinished.
        iii. But the Bridegroom is faithful.
    c. Emphasize:
        i. hope grows in the waiting
        ii. Christ is present in the middle
        iii. the future is secure because He is faithful
    d. **Optional closing line:** "We remain steady not because the world is certain, but because Christ is."

7. **Bridge to Week 5**
    a. You may conclude by noting: And Scripture ultimately tells us that this long season of preparation and waiting is moving toward something joyful, a great gathering where love is fully realized.

5

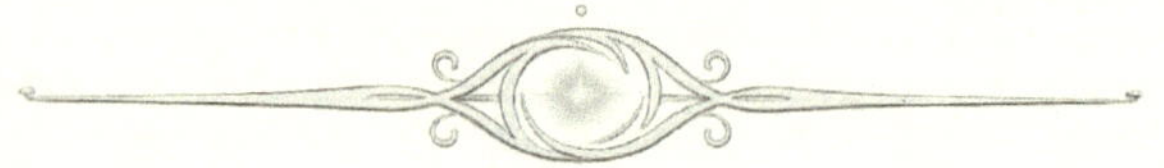

The Wedding Feast

Theological Themes & Ministry Connections

The Wedding Feast invites us into one of Scripture's most radiant images of the Christian hope. Unlike philosophical accounts of the afterlife – where the final state is imagined as escape, absorption, or disembodied serenity – the biblical vision is profoundly relational. At the center of all things is not an idea, nor a reward, nor a perfected self, but a *union*: the Bride and the Bridegroom sharing joy that overflows into the renewal of creation itself.

This image reveals something crucial about God's heart. The end of the story is not a courtroom, a battlefield, or even a throne room, but a table. A banquet. A celebration overflowing with abundance. What began in a garden ends in a feast – suggesting that divine love does not merely restore what was lost but brings it to fulfillment, beauty, and consummation.

Theologically, the Wedding Feast integrates two threads often kept separate in Christian teaching: eschatology and spiritual formation. Revelation's climactic vision of union ("The marriage supper of the Lamb has come") is not simply a future event–it is the telos that shapes Christian life in the present.[14] The Bride "makes herself ready," not by earning acceptance but by being transformed by love. The feast therefore becomes a lens for understanding sanctification: every act of obedience, every moment of surrender, every practice of love is a stitch in the garment the Bride will one day wear.

This offers a needed corrective to two common distortions. On one hand, some Christians imagine discipleship as a kind of grim persistence–faithfulness as duty without joy. On the other hand, popular religious culture often reduces heaven to sentimentality or vague comfort. The Wedding Feast cuts through both illusions. It tells us that Christian hope is neither stoic endurance nor spiritual escapism; it is preparation for a joy so weighty, so relational, so mutual, that it will require all of who we are. The feast forms desire. It shapes imagination. It pulls the believer forward through suffering with a vision strong enough to sustain hope.

---

[14] Hans Urs von Balthasar, Theo-Drama, Vol. V: The Last Act (San Francisco: Ignatius Press, 1998).

For ministry, this theme is particularly potent. Many people sit in church longing for purpose, for assurance, for a sense that their efforts and griefs are part of something larger. The Wedding Feast allows the preacher to give shape to that longing. It proclaims that history is not circling endlessly, nor is personal suffering meaningless. All of life–its waiting, its wounds, its work–is gathering toward a moment when joy will overflow and union will be complete. To preach the Wedding Feast, then, is to restore the imagination of hope: a hope that is communal, embodied, and radiant.

This theme also provides rich opportunities for pastoral connection. For those wrestling with grief, the vision of a feast where "death is swallowed up forever" offers a tenderness that mere argument cannot. For those who feel spiritually weary or inadequate, the image of the Bride being made ready by God Himself reframes the struggle: sanctification is not self-improvement; it is preparation for love. And for congregations longing for unity, the feast reminds them that the future God is preparing is not for individuals alone, but for a people made one in love.

The Wedding Feast is, ultimately, a vision meant to form us. It teaches the Church to live toward joy, to resist despair, to long for God without apology. It invites preachers and teachers to remind their congregations that Christianity is not merely a system of beliefs but a love story moving toward consummation. When proclaimed well, this theme does not draw attention to the preacher's insight but awakens the congregation's desire–so that they begin to sense, even now, the pulling of that great and future joy.

Context For Ministry

Your task in this part of the series is to expand the horizon of hope. Not with speculation, but with Scripture's own imagery. Not with escapism, but with transformation. Not with fear, but with invitation.

This is an opportunity to help your people see why their longings matter, why suffering does not have the last word, why the Christian life is a preparation, not an audition, why joy is not peripheral but central to salvation. And above all–why the Wedding Feast is not merely our future, but the light by which we interpret the present.

1. **Modern frameworks of meaning are shrinking.**
   Many people now imagine life as a closed system with no greater destination than personal fulfillment, comfort, or achievement. Without a larger story, hope becomes either sentimental ("things will work out") or utilitarian ("I hope this improves my life"). The result is a generation hungry for meaning yet unsure what kind of hope can sustain them.

2. **Scripture offers a radically different vision.**
   The biblical story does not culminate in escape, self-actualization, or solitary serenity. It ends with a feast–a communal, joyful, embodied celebration of union between Christ and His people. The wedding banquet is the image Jesus Himself uses to describe

ultimate reality. But in contemporary faith communities, few people know what to do with this imagery. For some, it feels symbolic but impractical; for others, overly mystical or distant. Many Christians simply have no robust imagination for eternity beyond clouds, harps, or vague bliss. Without a compelling eschatological vision, discipleship becomes fragile: people try to "be good" without knowing what they are being prepared for.

3. **Life looks different when it is shaped by a destination.** When a couple is engaged, everything bends toward the wedding day–not in anxiety but anticipation. Budgets shift, priorities change, conversations deepen, and both people grow in the direction of the life they will share. This is exactly the picture Scripture invites us to live into.

4. **The Wedding Feast gives clarity to Christian hope.** It tells us:
    a. The end of the story is not isolation but communion.
    b. The culmination of history is not destruction but celebration.
    c. Our future is not abstract union but embodied, relational joy.
    d. God is preparing a place for us–and preparing us for that place.

Many congregants have never heard this articulated with warmth, depth, or imagination. They know Christianity promises heaven, but they do not know heaven is described as a home filled with laughter, a table filled with abundance, a community made whole, and a love fully shared.

Biblical Commentary

- **Old Testament: Isaiah 25:6–9 – The Feast on the Mountain of the Lord**
  Isaiah paints one of Scripture's earliest and richest visions of the final union between God and His people: a banquet of abundance, the removal of shame, the swallowing up of death, and the wiping away of every tear. The image of a feast is not merely symbolic–it is deeply relational. God is not only hosting a banquet; He is giving Himself as the joy of His people. The emphasis on *all nations* anticipates the universal scope of Christ's redemptive work. In this passage, feasting becomes eschatological hope: the day when God Himself becomes the soul's satisfaction. It is the Old Testament root system for Jesus' parables and Revelation's Marriage Supper of the Lamb.

- **Gospel: Matthew 22:1–14 – The Parable of the Wedding Banquet**
  Jesus' parable reframes the kingdom of heaven as an invitation–one that many ignore, resist, or treat lightly. The tragedy of the story is not in the severity of judgment but in the refusal of joy. Those invited choose fields, businesses, and distractions over the

feast of the King's Son. The narrative exposes the misplaced loves of the human heart: we prefer the predictable, the manageable, and the self-directed over the abundance of God. The wedding garment, traditionally interpreted as righteousness or transformed desire, highlights the inner preparation required to participate in the feast. This parable positions the entire Christian life as an RSVP lived out over time.

- **Epistle: Ephesians 5:25–27 – Christ's Love Preparing His Bride**
  Paul presents the marriage metaphor not as a sentimental image but as a theological blueprint. Christ loves the Church with a purifying love–one that cleanses, forms, and beautifies until she is "without stain or wrinkle." The emphasis is not on human striving but on divine agency: Christ prepares His Bride through sanctifying love. The imagery reveals the telos of Christian formation: not mere improvement, but readiness for union. In this passage, holiness is marital–not moralism but communion made visible. The feast becomes possible because Christ has made His people lovely.

- **Eschatological Vision: Revelation 19:6–9 – The Marriage Supper of the Lamb**
  Here the biblical story reaches its climax: heaven rejoices because the wedding has come and "the Bride has made herself ready." The feast is not an end in itself, nor a reward for moral

achievement. It is the consummation of the relationship God has been initiating since creation–union fulfilled. The Bride's readiness is described as "fine linen, bright and clean," interpreted as "the righteous acts of the saints." Yet even these acts are given by grace; they are the clothing woven through divine-human cooperation. Revelation frames the Christian life not as survival, but as preparation for a joy so profound that heaven itself shouts with thunderous praise.

Homiletical & Exegetical Questions

Textual Questions

1. How does Revelation 19:6–9 use imagery from ancient Jewish wedding customs to illuminate the meaning of the marriage supper of the Lamb?
2. What is being emphasized when John writes, *"His Bride has made herself ready"*–and how does that readiness relate to both divine action and human participation?
3. In Matthew 22:1–14, what does the parable of the wedding banquet reveal about God's invitation, human response, and the seriousness of discipleship?
4. How does Isaiah 25:6–9 frame the feast as an act of divine victory, abundance, and tenderness?
5. What specific textual connections link the Wedding Feast to earlier biblical promises–covenant, betrothal, redemption, new creation?

Theological Questions

1. What does the Wedding Feast suggest about the nature of salvation–not merely rescue, but union and joy?
2. How does the eschatological vision of union reshape our understanding of sanctification in the present?
3. What does it mean that *joy* is at the center of Christian hope? How does this challenge common assumptions about the Christian life?
4. How does the imagery of a feast–embodied, communal, celebratory–counter overly spiritualized or disembodied visions of eternity?
5. What tensions arise between divine sovereignty ("it has been granted to her") and human preparation ("she has made herself ready")?

Pastoral Questions

1. How do people in your congregation imagine heaven? Is their imagination shaped more by culture or by Scripture?
2. What fears or wounds prevent people from believing that God desires joy, celebration, and intimacy with them?
3. How might the Wedding Feast speak into experiences of grief, loneliness, or disappointment?

4. What pastoral opportunities arise from proclaiming a future where the community of believers is gathered, healed, and united in love?
5. How can this theme encourage congregants who feel spiritually inadequate or weary?

Formational Questions

1. If life is preparation for union with Christ, what practices help the soul become attentive, receptive, and ready?
2. What "garments" (virtues, habits, desires) are being woven in the believer through ordinary faithfulness?
3. How might a sustained vision of the Wedding Feast reshape a congregation's imagination–toward joy, hope, and relational wholeness?
4. What does it mean to cultivate desire for God rather than duty or fear?
5. How can Christian community practice "foretastes" of the feast now–hospitality, celebration, shared life, generosity?

Suggested Sermon Flow

1. **Opening Vision: The Human Longing for Joyful Completion**
    a. **Goal:** Surface the universal experience of longing for things to be made whole.

b. You may begin by observing:
   i. Throughout life, people look forward to moments of meaningful completion.
   ii. There is something deeply human about anticipating a joyful gathering after a long season of effort or waiting.
   iii. Scripture speaks directly into this longing.
c. Gently connect: The Christian story does not end in strain or uncertainty, but in celebration.
d. **Tone:** warm, hopeful, grounded.
e. **Optional transition line:** "The Bible repeatedly describes the future God is preparing as a feast."

2. **Human Experience Bridge: Why Feasts Mark the Most Important Moments**
   a. **Goal:** Ground the imagery in lived human experience.
   b. You might note:
      i. Across cultures and centuries, feasts have marked moments of covenant, reconciliation, and joy.
      ii. Shared meals often signal belonging and restored relationship.
      iii. Weddings, in particular, have long culminated in communal celebration.
   c. You may briefly acknowledge: While cultural expressions vary, the human instinct to celebrate love through shared table fellowship remains deeply familiar.

   d. **Pastoral sensitivity:** Keep the tone inclusive and humane; avoid sentimental excess.
   e. **Transition:** "This helps us hear the richness of the imagery Scripture uses."

3. **Scriptural Illumination: Blessed Are Those Invited**
   a. **Goal:** Let the biblical texts carry the emotional and theological weight.
   b. Guide the congregation through the passages, highlighting:
      i. Revelation's announcement of the wedding supper
      ii. Isaiah's vision of the feast prepared by God
      iii. Jesus' affirmation of faithful servants entering joy
   c. Key themes to surface:
      i. divine initiative in preparing the feast
      ii. the joy set before God's people
      iii. the communal nature of salvation
      iv. the faithfulness of God to complete the story
   d. **Important:** Allow the texts to breathe; avoid over-systematizing.
4. **Pastoral Clarification: Joy Without Escapism**
   a. **Goal:** Prevent common misunderstandings.
   b. Gently clarify that the biblical vision of the feast is **not**:
      i. escapism from the world
      ii. denial of present suffering
      iii. emotional triumphalism

iv. reward for spiritual performance

c. Rather, it is:

i. the faithful completion of God's long work

ii. the fulfillment of covenant love

iii. the healing of what has been fractured

iv. the joy of shared life with Christ

d. **Tone:** steady, theologically grounded, pastorally wise.

5. Formational Invitation: Living Now in Light of the Coming Joy

a. **Goal:** Offer grounded life application.

b. You may invite the congregation to reflect:

i. How might this promised joy reshape our present faithfulness?

ii. Where is Christ already inviting us to live with quiet hope?

iii. What would it look like to practice gratitude even now?

c. Encourage simple responses such as:

i. practicing thankfulness in ordinary moments

ii. extending generosity to others

iii. living with patient expectancy

iv. remaining faithful in small things

d. **Important:** Keep the invitation gentle and hope-filled.

6. Closing Image: The Table That Is Being Prepared

a. **Goal:** Leave the congregation with peaceful, joyful anticipation.
b. Return to the wedding imagery:
    i. The table is being set.
    ii. The Bride is being prepared.
    iii. The Bridegroom is faithful.
c. Emphasize:
    i. the future is secure in Christ
    ii. the waiting is purposeful
    iii. the joy ahead is real
d. **Optional closing line:** "Blessed indeed are those who are invited to the wedding supper of the Lamb."

7. **Bridge Beyond the Series (Optional Pastoral Close)**
    a. Since this concludes the arc, you may gently encourage:
        i. The invitation of Christ is not only future, it shapes how we live even now, as a people learning to belong more fully to Him.
    b. This allows pastors flexibility to:
        i. end the series
        ii. move into application
        iii. or transition into another teaching focus

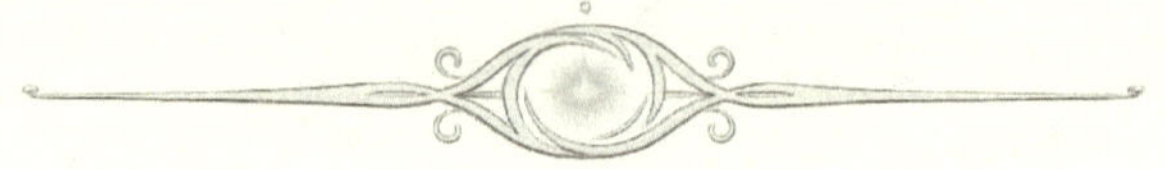

Theological Foundations for the Practices in these Resources

Why Contemplative Practices Matter

Across many congregations today, leaders sense a quiet tension. Believers have access to more biblical information than at any time in history, yet many still struggle to experience a settled, attentive life with God. Sermons are heard, studies are completed, and yet the deeper formation of the heart often unfolds more slowly than we might hope.[15]

The practices included in the *Bride of Christ* series are offered in response to that pastoral reality. They are not presented as innovations or replacements for the ordinary means of grace. Rather, they are gentle

[15] Thomas Merton, New Seeds of Contemplation (New York: New Directions, 1961).

supports designed to help God's people attend more fully to the Word they are already receiving and the presence of Christ already promised to them.

Throughout the history of the Church, seasons of renewal have often included a recovery of unhurried attentiveness before God. These practices stand within that historic contemplative stream of the Christian Church, which has quietly formed believers across many traditions for centuries. Properly understood, they do not move believers away from Scripture, but more deeply into it – not away from congregational life, but more faithfully within it.

For pastors and ministry leaders, the aim is simple: to create spaces in which the Word of God can be received not only with clarity of mind, but with openness of heart and steadiness of attention.

Silence in the Biblical Witness

Silence in Scripture is not emptiness but expectancy. Again and again, the biblical narrative portrays the people of God growing attentive in moments where noise and urgency give way to stillness.

The psalmist writes, "Be still, and know that I am God" (Psalm 46:10). Elijah encounters the Lord not in the wind, earthquake, or fire, but in the "low whisper" (1 Kings 19:12). Habakkuk calls the earth to quiet reverence before the Lord (Habakkuk 2:20). Even in the Gospels, Jesus repeatedly withdraws to solitary places to pray (Luke 5:16).

These patterns remind us that silence has long served the life of faith not as an end in itself, but as a posture of attentiveness. The purpose is never withdrawal for its own sake, but receptivity – a willingness to become present to God in a world that often trains us toward distraction.

In congregational settings, brief, guided moments of shared quiet can help modern believers rediscover this biblical posture. When framed pastorally and practiced gently, silence becomes not an unfamiliar technique but a recovery of something deeply rooted in the life of prayer.

Breath and Prayer in the Christian Tradition

Scripture presents breath as a gift intimately connected to the life God gives. Humanity comes to life as God breathes into Adam the breath of life (Genesis 2:7). The risen Christ breathes on His disciples as a sign of the Spirit's presence among them (John 20:22). Breath, in the biblical imagination, is never merely mechanical; it is bound up with creaturely dependence and divine gift.

The gentle breathing practices included in this series are therefore not presented as techniques for altered states or heightened experience. Rather, they serve a simple pastoral purpose: helping the body grow calm enough for the heart and mind to attend more fully to God in prayer.

Many believers today carry significant physical tension and mental distraction into times of worship and reflection. Slow, attentive breathing can help participants settle without strain, creating a more receptive posture for hearing Scripture. Leaders should present these moments simply and without emphasis on performance. The goal is not mastery of breath, but quiet readiness before the Lord.

Lectio Divina and Sacred Reading

The slow, repeated reading of Scripture practiced in this series reflects the historic Christian discipline commonly known as *lectio divina*, or "sacred reading." Emerging in the early monastic tradition and described classically by Guigo II in *The Ladder of Monks*, this approach to Scripture emphasizes listening for the living voice of God through the biblical text.[16]

At its heart, this practice assumes something deeply biblical: that the Word of God is not merely information to be analyzed, but living speech to be received (Hebrews 4:12). The repeated, unhurried reading of a passage allows space for the Spirit to bring particular phrases or images gently to the attention of the listener.

---

[16] Guigo II, The Ladder of Monks, trans. Edmund Colledge and James Walsh (Kalamazoo, MI: Cistercian Publications, 1981).

In pastoral settings, this approach does not replace careful exegesis or doctrinal teaching. Rather, it complements them by helping congregants internalize Scripture devotionally as well as intellectually. Leaders are encouraged to keep the tone simple, Scripture-centered, and free from interpretive pressure. The aim is attentive listening, not forced insight.

Posture, Attention, and the Whole-Person Life of Prayer

Christian prayer has always involved the whole person. Scripture describes believers kneeling (Ephesians 3:14), lifting hands (Psalm 63:4), bowing in worship (Psalm 95:6), and standing in reverence (Nehemiah 9:5). These embodied expressions remind us that discipleship is not merely mental assent but lived, physical devotion.

The practices in this series occasionally invite participants to notice posture, stillness, or gentle physical awareness. These invitations are intentionally modest. They are not techniques to be perfected, but simple ways of helping modern believers – often accustomed to constant motion – rediscover a settled attentiveness before God.

Leaders should emphasize freedom and gentleness. Participants may adapt posture as needed for comfort and physical limitation. What matters is not precision of form, but the cultivation of a receptive, prayerful presence before the Lord.

A Pastoral Word to Leaders

As you guide your congregation through these practices, remember that they are offered as supports, not requirements. They do not replace the central work of preaching the Word, administering the sacraments, or shepherding the people of God. Rather, they are meant to serve that work by helping congregations become more attentive, receptive, and spiritually present.

Some participants may find the slower pace unfamiliar at first. Others may enter the rhythm quickly. In either case, your calm and confident leadership will set the tone. There is no need to force outcomes or manufacture particular experiences. The Spirit of God is already at work among His people.

Use these practices with pastoral wisdom. Adapt them where needed. Keep Scripture central, Christ clearly proclaimed, and the atmosphere marked by gentleness rather than urgency.

The Bridegroom who calls His Church is patient and faithful. As you lead, trust that the quiet work of formation often unfolds in ways that are steady, hidden, and deeply fruitful over time.

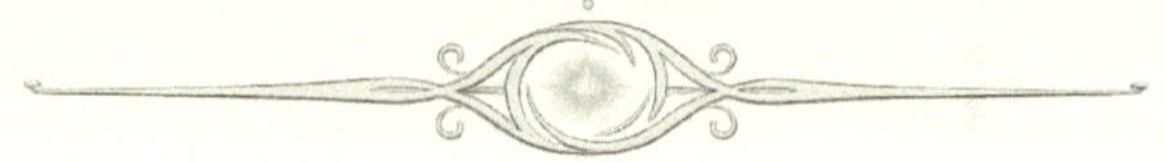

Recommended Reading & Research

This curated selection of texts provides pastors, priests, ministry leaders, and teachers with a deeper well from which to draw. These works span biblical studies, patristic theology, contemplative spirituality, eschatology, and pastoral formation. Each title is chosen for its resonance with the themes explored in the series: divine union, spiritual preparation, covenantal faithfulness, hope in suffering, and the consummation of all things in Christ.

Scriptural Theology & Biblical Studies

N. T. Wright

- **Surprised by Hope**: A clear theological foundation for Christian eschatology, resurrection, and new creation.

- **Paul for Everyone: 1 Corinthians & 2 Corinthians**: Helpful commentary on themes of transformation, glory, and union.

Richard B. Hays

- **Echoes of Scripture in the Gospels**: Excellent for tracing Old Testament bridal and covenant themes into the Gospels.

G. K. Beale

- **The Book of Revelation (NIGTC Commentary)**: Deep theological exploration of Revelation's imagery, including the Marriage Supper of the Lamb.

Raymond E. Brown

- **The Gospel According to John**: Insightful treatment of Johannine themes of abiding, love, glory, and union.

Christopher J. H. Wright

- **Knowing Jesus Through the Old Testament**: Helpful for tracing how OT covenantal imagery is fulfilled in Christ.

Patristic & Medieval Sources

St. Augustine

- **Confessions:** A foundational text on desire, love, and the restless heart's union with God.

St. Bernard of Clairvaux

- **On Loving God & Sermons on the Song of Songs:** Vital for understanding bridal spirituality and the soul's movement toward union.

St. John of the Cross

- **The Spiritual Canticle & Dark Night of the Soul:** Poetic and theological reflections on the purification of desire and the journey into divine intimacy.

St. Teresa of Ávila

- **Interior Castle:** A map of spiritual maturity and union with Christ.

Modern Contemplative & Spiritual Formation Writers

Thomas Merton

- **New Seeds of Contemplation**: A pastoral exploration of identity, union, desire, and contemplation.
- **The Seven Storey Mountain**: A narrative of awakening and surrender helpful for teaching spiritual formation.

Thomas Keating

- **Invitation to Love** – A practical framework for understanding transformation and removal of the false self.
- **Open Mind, Open Heart** – Insights into contemplative prayer as preparation for union.

Henri Nouwen

- **The Return of the Prodigal Son** – Powerful reflections on identity, love, and spiritual belonging.
- **Lifesigns** – Contemplation on fear, love, and trust as foundations of Christian spirituality.

Dallas Willard

- **Renovation of the Heart** – A clear and pastoral exposition of spiritual formation into Christlikeness.

Eschatology, Hope, & Christian Imagination

Jürgen Moltmann

- **The Coming of God:** A profound theological exploration of eschatological hope.

Hans Urs von Balthasar

- **Theo-Drama, Vol. V: The Last Act:** Provides rich imagery for understanding the consummation of all things in divine love.

C. S. Lewis

- **The Great Divorce** – A theological parable of desire, choice, and the soul's journey toward God.
- **The Weight of Glory** – Reflections on the glory to be revealed in us.

Marriage, Covenant, & Spirituality

Timothy Keller

- **The Meaning of Marriage:** Helpful insights on covenant love and self-giving that parallel the theological themes of the series.

John Paul II

- **Man and Woman He Created Them: A Theology of the Body:** Deep theology of embodiment, desire, self-gift, and relational union.

Mike Mason

- **The Mystery of Marriage:** A poetic, contemplative reflection on marriage as a spiritual discipline.

Pastoral Tools for Practice & Formation

Jim Nestor

- **Breathe:** Teachings on breathwork, relaxation, and embodiment for contemplative prayer.

Adele Ahlberg Calhoun

- **Spiritual Disciplines Handbook:** A practical guide for integrating disciplines of surrender, silence, love, and devotion.

Ruth Haley Barton

- **Sacred Rhythms:** Accessible and pastoral introduction to spiritual formation practices.

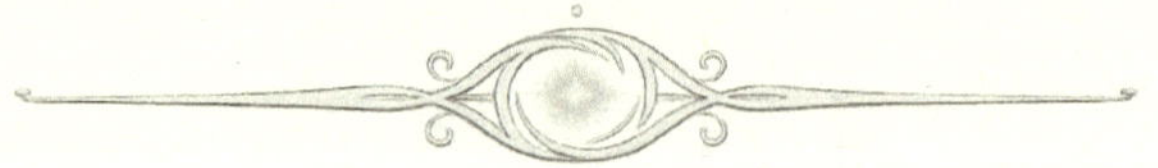

Thank You for Walking This Journey

You have completed the series, *The Bride of Christ.* This guide was crafted for leaders who seek to help people, not only to learn about God, but to encounter Him. If something within you has stirred, softened, or awakened during these weeks, give thanks: the Spirit is already shaping you into the image of Christ.

Continue Growing with Symbol & Silence

Symbol & Silence exists to help Christians explore the depths of Scripture with clarity, humility, and contemplative joy. Each week, new essays and reflections are published on Substack – always free, always accessible.

To learn more or to join, visit: http://www.symbolandsilence.com where you will find Bible studies, devotionals, pastoral resources, ministry guides, artwork, and teaching tools.

May your leadership create spaces where the people of God learn to listen, abide, and grow in responsive love to Christ.

www.ingramcontent.com/pod-product-compliance
Lightning Source LLC
LaVergne TN
LVHW051014080826
845145LV00009B/2612

* 9 7 8 1 9 7 2 0 8 8 0 2 9 *